Amphibian Rescue

Vickie An

Smithsonian

Contributing Author

Allison Duarte, M.A.

Consultants

Tamieka Grizzle, Ed.D.
K–5 STEM Lab Instructor
Harmony Leland Elementary School

Brian Gratwicke, Ph.D.
Conservation Biologist
Smithsonian National Zoo

Publishing Credits

Rachelle Cracchiolo, M.S.Ed., *Publisher*
Conni Medina, M.A.Ed., *Managing Editor*
Diana Kenney, M.A.Ed., NBCT, *Content Director*
Véronique Bos, *Creative Director*
June Kikuchi, *Content Director*
Robin Erickson, Art Director
Seth Rogers, *Editor*
Mindy Duits, *Senior Graphic Designer*
Smithsonian Science Education Center

Image Credits: front cover, p.1 Steven David Miller/Minden Images; p.5 (top) Joel Sartore/National Geographic/Getty Images; p.7 Stephen Dalton/Minden Pictures/Newscom; pp.8–9 Erik McGregor/Pacific Press/Newscom; p.10 Danté Fenolio/Science Source; p.11 John Cancalosi/Alamy; p.12, p.13, p.17 (right), p.18, p.19, p.22, p.24, p.25, p.26, p.27, p.28, p.32 © Smithsonian; p.14 Fabio Pupin/FLPA imageBroker/Newscom; p.15 Emanuele Biggi/FLPA imageBroker/Newscom; p.21 Matt McClain/For The Washington Post via Getty Images; p.23 Chris Austin, LSU Supplied by WENN/Newsom; all other images from iStock and/or Shutterstock.

Library of Congress Cataloging-in-Publication Data

Names: An, Vickie, author.
Title: Amphibian rescue / Vickie An.
Description: Huntington Beach, CA : Teacher Created Materials, [2018] | Audience: K to grade 3. | Includes index.
Identifiers: LCCN 2017056316 (print) | LCCN 2018004601 (ebook) | ISBN 9781493869176 (e-book) | ISBN 9781493866779 (pbk.)
Subjects: LCSH: Frogs--Conservation--Juvenile literature. | Amphibians--Conservation--Juvenile literature. | Amphibians--Juvenile literature.
Classification: LCC QL668.E2 (ebook) | LCC QL668.E2 A49 2018 (print) | DDC 333.95/78--dc23
LC record available at https://lccn.loc.gov/2017056316

Smithsonian

Teacher Created Materials

5301 Oceanus Drive
Huntington Beach, CA 92649-1030
www.tcmpub.com

ISBN 978-1-4938-6677-9

Printed by: 590835
Printed in: China

Table of Contents

Awesome Amphibians 4

A Vanishing Act 6

The Fight for Frogs 12

Building a Safe Home 18

Making Leaps! 26

STEAM Challenge... 28

Glossary 30

Index 31

Career Advice.. 32

Awesome Amphibians

Frogs, toads, newts (NOOTS), and salamanders are pretty amazing. Did you know that frogs and toads use their eyes to push down food when they swallow? Did you know that salamanders and newts can grow new **limbs**? There are also some frogs that can jump 20 times their body length. But, all of these animals have something in common. They are all **amphibians** (am-FIH-bee-uhnz).

Amphibians comes from Greek words. *Amphi* means "two" or "both." *Bios* means "life." Amphibians lead two lives. Most spend part of their lives in water. But they also spend time living on land.

Amphibians can be found all over the world. They live in streams, rain forests, deserts, and everywhere in between. There are more than 7,500 kinds of amphibians. Many of them are in danger. But help is on the way.

Tadpoles grow up to be frogs that live on land.

The Chinese giant salamander is the biggest amphibian in the world. It can grow up to 1.8 meters (6 feet) long.

Red-spotted newts are amphibians.

A Vanishing Act

Scientists are worried about amphibians. More than 120 kinds of frogs and salamanders have gone **extinct** in the past 40 years. That means they have all died. They no longer exist. Nearly half of all amphibian **species** are at risk. Now, there's a race to save them.

Almost all amphibians have thin, moist (MOYST) skin. They drink through their skin. Their skin also helps them breathe. This makes them sensitive to their surroundings. Even a slight rise in temperature can have a big effect on amphibians.

Hot weather can lead to droughts (DROWTS). These are long periods of no rain. Ponds and swamps dry up. Most amphibians lay their eggs in water. When ponds dry up, they have no place to go.

A frog lays its eggs.

Frogs have tongues that attach to the fronts of their mouths, not the backs like humans. When they hunt, they flip out their tongues to catch food.

More Troubles

Loss of habitat is another problem. A habitat is the home of an animal. Humans are destroying the areas where amphibians live. They are cutting down forests and draining **wetlands**. They want to use the land to build houses, farms, and shops. New buildings take the place of swamps and ponds. As a result, amphibians are losing their homes. Frogs have had it especially hard.

Why Does It Matter?

A decrease in the number of frogs can cause big problems. Frogs play a key role in the food chain. They eat all kinds of insects. Imagine how many more bugs would be buzzing around if not for frogs. Frogs are also food for birds, reptiles, and mammals. Plus, frogs tell us a great deal about the health of an environment. How? When they start dying in large numbers, it's a sign that something is wrong.

Amphibians are cold-blooded. This means they cannot control their body temperature on their own. Amphibians often warm themselves by sitting in the sun.

Construction damages these wetlands.

A frog eats an insect.

One of the biggest dangers frogs face is from a **fungus**. This deadly fungus is called *chytrid* (KIH-trihd). It infects the skin. The fungus can spread by touching infected skin. It can also be spread through water. The disease moves fast. It has killed dozens of frog species. Hundreds more may soon be gone, too.

No one knows where the fungus came from. Humans transport frogs all over the world. The fungus could have come from anywhere. Some people think it is from Africa. It might have spread from there since many labs use African clawed frogs for research. Other people think American bullfrogs are to blame. Their legs are served in restaurants around the world. Wherever the fungus is from, it is now found almost everywhere frogs live.

The lemur tree frog is one species threatened by the chytrid fungus.

This wood frog may have died from the chytrid fungus.

SCIENCE

A Fungus Among Us

Chytrid changes a frog's skin. Since a frog breathes and drinks through its skin, an infected frog can die within months.

The Fight for Frogs

Scientists are not giving up on frogs. Some of them are working to save frogs in Panama. Panama is in Central America. It has a warm, wet climate. A large part of the country is covered in rain forests, **cloud forests**, and wetlands. More than two hundred species of amphibians live in Panama.

Sadly, it is too late for some frogs. Some species have not been seen in years. Panama's harlequin (HAHR-lih-kwihn) frogs and glass frogs are in trouble, too. These are just a few of the frogs that the chytrid fungus has harmed. But there is still hope. Scientists have opened a rescue lab. It is the biggest of its kind.

A young woman works at a rescue lab for amphibians in Panama.

The skin of one Panamanian golden frog contains enough poison to kill 1,200 mice.

To collect frogs, teams of researchers go into the wild. They go to places where they think the fungus has not reached. They know that the fungus spreads through water. Research shows that it grows faster in cooler weather, too. So, frogs that live in cool mountain streams are most at risk.

No special traps are needed to catch the frogs. Instead, scientists use something that can be found in most kitchens. Here is a hint: People use them to pack sandwiches for their lunches. That's right! Scientists put frogs in plastic bags. They are very careful not to touch the frogs. Scientists write when and where the frogs were found. Then, they take them to the rescue center.

A scientist studies a marsh frog.

Most of Panama was covered in rain forest until the Panama Canal was built in the twentieth century.

A scientist collects a sample from a frog.

Frogs can be very hard to find. Many have natural **camouflage** (KA-muh-flahj). They blend in with their habitat. This keeps them safe from **predators**.

So, instead of using their eyes, scientists use their ears. They can identify frogs from their calls. Each frog species makes a **unique** sound. It can be easy to know which frog is nearby if you know the sounds that it makes.

Like humans, frogs have vocal cords. They also have a vocal sac below their mouths. This sac fills with air and makes their calls louder. Some frogs can be heard 1.6 kilometers (1 mile) away. The frogs use their calls to attract **mates**, call for help, and scare off predators. They can sound like croaks, clicks, or whistles. There are even some species that sound like they are barking!

A tree frog prepares to call out.

poison arrow frog

spiny-headed tree frog

ARTS

Hide and Seek

Blending in is just one way that frogs use camouflage. Others do the opposite. Some frogs use **mimicry** (MIH-mih-kree) to stay safe. This is when a frog makes itself look more dangerous than it is. Some harmless frogs have learned to mimic the bright colors of poisonous frogs that live nearby. Their bright colors warn that they are deadly even though they aren't.

Building a Safe Home

Back at the lab, a lot of teamwork goes into caring for the frogs. Veterinarians make sure the frogs stay healthy. Scientists watch the frogs to learn about their behavior. Researchers study the fungus. Together, they learn more about frogs.

The rescue lab has three main parts. The first is a working lab for the researchers. The second is where the frogs are kept right after being brought from the wild. Here, frogs are watched to make sure they are not sick. Finally, there are the rescue pods. In all, the seven pods hold 12 endangered frog species.

Rescue lab workers make baths to help frogs fight chytrid.

There are many tanks in each rescue pod.

MATHEMATICS

How Many Frogs?

Designers had to plan for the number of frog habitats that could fit in each rescue pod. First, they measured the length of the pods. Next, they measured the length of the tanks used for the frog habitats. Finally, they divided the total length of the pods by the total length of the tanks. This told them the number of habitat tanks that could fit in each rescue pod.

When frogs arrive, they are tested for the chytrid fungus right away. If a frog is sick, it is given medicine. It is also cleaned with a special liquid. To be extra safe, it is kept away from other frogs for 30 days. This is called *quarantine*. The frog is then moved into a habitat made just for it. The environment in the lab must be perfect for the frogs to survive. It cannot be too hot or too cold. The humidity, or level of moisture in the air, must be just right. The amount of light is important, too.

As the pods fill, there are many hungry mouths to feed. Scientists raise all the food that the frogs eat. Crickets and fruit flies make up most of the menu.

A frog eats a fly.

A scientist holds a container with a frog.

ENGINEERING

Reuse and Recycle

There are seven rescue pods at the lab in Panama. These new frog homes are built from old shipping containers. They were once used to move frozen goods all around the world. Engineers designed them to be used as mini-ecosystems for the frogs.

In some cases, the frogs at the research center are the last of their kind. One mission of the project is to breed the frogs. *Breed* means "to make offspring, or young." Scientists hope this will help save the species. So, if these frogs go extinct in the wild, the species will not be lost completely.

Scientists already have one win. They successfully bred a species of poison dart frog. The little froglet was the first of its kind to be hatched by humans. It is smaller than a dime! It was first discovered in Panama in 2014. These breeding programs have a goal. That goal is to release the frogs back to the wild some day.

blue poison dart frog

The world's smallest amphibian is a tiny frog species called *Paedophryne amauensis* (PAY-doh-freen ah-mow-EN-sis). It is about the size of a housefly!

Researchers are working hard to solve the chytrid fungus problem. At first, they thought bacteria might help. There are good kinds and bad kinds of bacteria. The bad kinds can make you sick. But the good kinds can keep you healthy. Scientists tested the good kinds on the frogs. These bacteria were known to fight fungus. Could one of them save the frogs from the chytrid fungus?

One study looked at the Panamanian golden frog. Scientists tried putting the bacteria on the frogs' skin. Nothing worked. Then, they got some good news. In one test, some golden frogs were able to fight off the fungus. But it was not due to the bacteria used in the test. It was because of the mix of bacteria already living on the frogs' skin. More work still needs to be done to find an answer.

Panamanian golden frog with eggs

The Panamanian golden frog is extinct in the wild. Today, the frog only exists in labs and zoos.

Making Leaps!

Today, scientists in Panama still fight for frogs. The research lab recently took an exciting step. They released 90 harlequin frogs into the rain forest. The frogs were bred in the rescue lab. They want to see whether frogs raised by humans can live in the wild. Researchers will track them every day. They hope the study will help save the species. Maybe it can save others, too.

Scientists will keep looking for a cure for the chytrid fungus. The rescue lab has made a safe home for 12 endangered frog species. This will help keep some alive until they can solve the problem. For now, we will have to wait and see whether the frogs can be saved.

These frogs wait to be released into the rain forest.

TECHNOLOGY

High-Tech Tracking

Some harlequin frogs were released wearing tiny radios. The radios helped scientists track the frogs. It was one of the first times they had been made for animals this small. The radios were tied around the frogs with a thin cord that fell off after a month. This was so the radios would fall off the frogs after the batteries died.

STEAM CHALLENGE

Define the Problem

Scientists in Panama want to develop another tool to catch frogs in the wild. They found that the chytrid fungus spreads to scientists' skin too easily with the current method. Can you create a safe and effective tool?

Constraints: Your design must be created using everyday household items and materials.

Criteria: You will test your design by using the tool to collect an object in and around a water tank.

Research and Brainstorm

Where do scientists collect the frogs? What do scientists currently use to collect frogs? What are the most important parts of a tool to catch frogs?

Design and Build

Sketch the design of your tool. What purpose will each part serve? What materials will work best? Build the model.

Test and Improve

Use your tool to collect an object. Did it work? How can you improve your tool? Modify your design, and try again.

Reflect and Share

Is the model strong enough to be used again? What other materials could you use to make a tool? Could the scientists use this tool for something else?

Glossary

amphibians—cold-blooded animals that are able to live on land and in water

camouflage—a way to hide by disguise

cloud forests—wet mountain forests that usually have many clouds

extinct—no longer existing

fungus—living thing that is not a plant or animal and lives in or on plants, animals, or decaying matter

limbs—arms, legs, or wings

mates—animals that are used for breeding

mimicry—protection from danger where an animal copies the coloring, look, or behavior of a more harmful animal

predators—animals that live by killing and eating other animals

species—a group of plants or animals that are similar and can produce young

unique—unlike anything else; special or unusual

wetlands—land or areas, such as swamps, having much soil moisture

Index

Africa, 10

African clawed frogs, 10

American bullfrogs, 10

camouflage, 16–17

Central America, 12

Chinese giant salamander, 5

chytrid fungus, 10–12, 14–15, 18, 20, 24, 26, 28

glass frogs, 12

habitat, 8, 16, 19–20

harlequin frogs, 12, 26–27

mimicry, 17

Paedophryne amauensis, 23

Panama, 12, 15, 21–22, 24, 26, 28

Panama Canal, 15

Panamanian golden frog, 13, 24–25

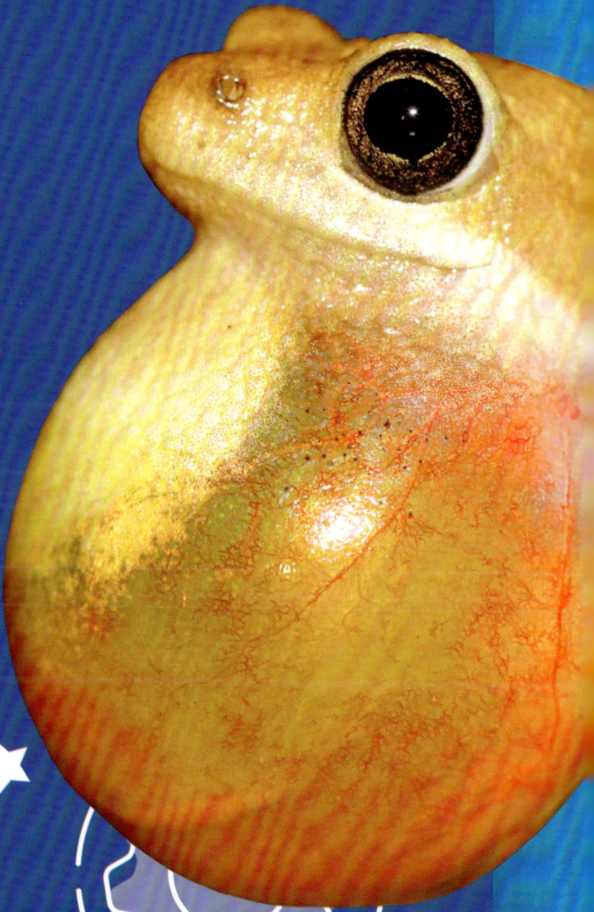

CAREER ADVICE
from Smithsonian

Do you want to help amphibians?
Here are some tips to get you started.

"As a kid, I loved reptiles and amphibians. This interest in herpetology stayed with me through high school and college, and now it's my career! Study biology and zoology, and spend time observing amphibians in their natural habitats. I learn something new about the animals I study all the time." **—Brian Gratwicke, Ph.D., Conservation Biologist**

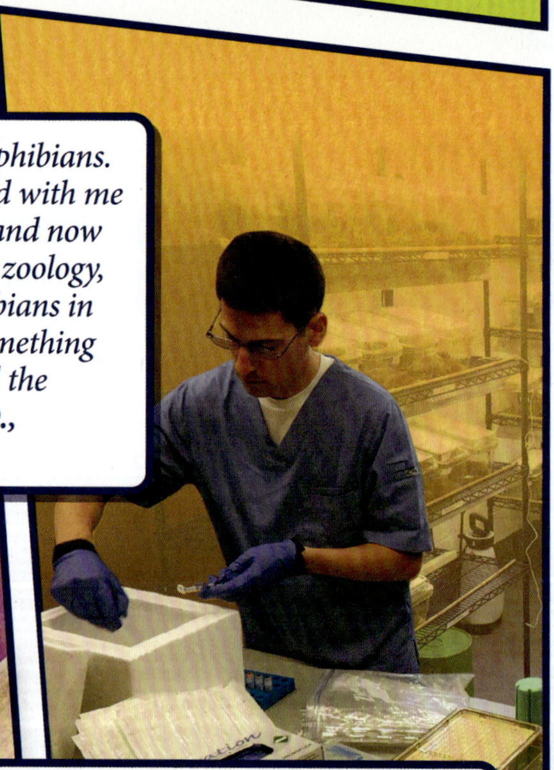

"It is an honor to work with an endangered species like the Panamanian golden frog. Taking care of these frogs means understanding their habitat and what they need to survive. It makes me feel good that I am doing something to help. If you love science, roaming outside, and being curious about nature, then you can help endangered frogs, too." **—Matt Evans, Biologist**